Web Log and Web Accounts

A Family Research Workbook

Written by Catherine Coulter

Books Written By Catherine Coulter

My Family Tree Research Records

Family Group Research Records

Census Research Records

Cemetery and Funeral Home Research Records

Court House Records Research Records

Web Log and Web Accounts

Books Written by Catherine Coulter under the name of Cathy Coulter

The Man in Red

A Children's Book of Poems Goodnight and Hello

Web Log

In This book you will be able to keep track of the many web sites that you use in your family tree research. In the Web Log you have a place to write in the web address, the names of the ancestors you want to use the web site for, your ancestor's birth date, death date, and spouse's name. These facts will help you in searching the web site. It will help you to Keep track of the ancestors you looked for or still need to look for on these sites.

Web Accounts

The Web Accounts page is to help you keep track of the web sites that you have accounts with or need to log on to in order to use. It has a place for you to write down the web site, your user name, password, and the dollar amount ($) you are charged to use the site if any. It also has a place for you to write down if it is a daily, monthly, or yearly payment, the date you started the account, and the date you ended the account. The dates will help you keep track of how long you used the web site and to document that you ended the account.

Web Log

Web Site:

Ancestor's Name	Birth Date	Death Date	Spouse

Web Site:

Ancestor's Name	Birth Date	Death Date	Spouse

Web Log

Web Site:			
Ancestor's Name	Birth Date	Death Date	Spouse

Web Site:			
Ancestor's Name	Birth Date	Death Date	Spouse

Web Log

Web Site:

Ancestor's Name	Birth Date	Death Date	Spouse

Web Site:

Ancestor's Name	Birth Date	Death Date	Spouse

Web Log

Web Site:			
Ancestor's Name	Birth Date	Death Date	Spouse

Web Site:			
Ancestor's Name	Birth Date	Death Date	Spouse

Web Log

Web Site:			
Ancestor's Name	Birth Date	Death Date	Spouse

Web Site:			
Ancestor's Name	Birth Date	Death Date	Spouse

Web Log

Web Site:			
Ancestor's Name	Birth Date	Death Date	Spouse

Web Site:			
Ancestor's Name	Birth Date	Death Date	Spouse

Web Log

Web Site:			
Ancestor's Name	Birth Date	Death Date	Spouse

Web Site:			
Ancestor's Name	Birth Date	Death Date	Spouse

Web Log

Web Site:			
Ancestor's Name	Birth Date	Death Date	Spouse

Web Site:			
Ancestor's Name	Birth Date	Death Date	Spouse

Web Log

Web Site:			
Ancestor's Name	Birth Date	Death Date	Spouse

Web Site:			
Ancestor's Name	Birth Date	Death Date	Spouse

Web Log

Web Site:			
Ancestor's Name	Birth Date	Death Date	Spouse

Web Site:			
Ancestor's Name	Birth Date	Death Date	Spouse

Web Log

Web Site:			
Ancestor's Name	Birth Date	Death Date	Spouse

Web Site:			
Ancestor's Name	Birth Date	Death Date	Spouse

Web Log

Web Site:			
Ancestor's Name	Birth Date	Death Date	Spouse

Web Site:			
Ancestor's Name	Birth Date	Death Date	Spouse

Web Log

Web Site:			
Ancestor's Name	Birth Date	Death Date	Spouse

Web Site:			
Ancestor's Name	Birth Date	Death Date	Spouse

Web Log

Web Site:			
Ancestor's Name	Birth Date	Death Date	Spouse

Web Site:			
Ancestor's Name	Birth Date	Death Date	Spouse

Web Log

Web Site:			
Ancestor's Name	Birth Date	Death Date	Spouse

Web Site:			
Ancestor's Name	Birth Date	Death Date	Spouse

Web Log

Web Site:			
Ancestor's Name	Birth Date	Death Date	Spouse

Web Site:			
Ancestor's Name	Birth Date	Death Date	Spouse

Web Log

Web Site:			
Ancestor's Name	Birth Date	Death Date	Spouse

Web Site:			
Ancestor's Name	Birth Date	Death Date	Spouse

Web Log

Web Site:			
Ancestor's Name	Birth Date	Death Date	Spouse

Web Site:			
Ancestor's Name	Birth Date	Death Date	Spouse

Web Log

Web Site:

Ancestor's Name	Birth Date	Death Date	Spouse

Web Site:

Ancestor's Name	Birth Date	Death Date	Spouse

Web Log

Web Site:			
Ancestor's Name	Birth Date	Death Date	Spouse

Web Site:			
Ancestor's Name	Birth Date	Death Date	Spouse

Web Accounts

Web Site:

User Name	Password	$	Day Monthly Yearly	Start Date	End Date

Web Site:

User Name	Password	$	Day Monthly Yearly	Start Date	End Date

Web Site:

User Name	Password	$	Day Monthly Yearly	Start Date	End Date

Web Site:

User Name	Password	$	Day Monthly Yearly	Start Date	End Date

Web Site:

User Name	Password	$	Day Monthly Yearly	Start Date	End Date

Web Site:

User Name	Password	$	Day Monthly Yearly	Start Date	End Date

Web Site:

User Name	Password	$	Day Monthly Yearly	Start Date	End Date

Web Accounts

Web Site:

User Name	Password	$	Day Monthly Yearly	Start Date	End Date

Web Site:

User Name	Password	$	Day Monthly Yearly	Start Date	End Date

Web Site:

User Name	Password	$	Day Monthly Yearly	Start Date	End Date

Web Site:

User Name	Password	$	Day Monthly Yearly	Start Date	End Date

Web Site:

User Name	Password	$	Day Monthly Yearly	Start Date	End Date

Web Site:

User Name	Password	$	Day Monthly Yearly	Start Date	End Date

Web Site:

User Name	Password	$	Day Monthly Yearly	Start Date	End Date

Web Accounts

Web Site:

User Name	Password	$	Day Monthly Yearly	Start Date	End Date

Web Site:

User Name	Password	$	Day Monthly Yearly	Start Date	End Date

Web Site:

User Name	Password	$	Day Monthly Yearly	Start Date	End Date

Web Site:

User Name	Password	$	Day Monthly Yearly	Start Date	End Date

Web Site:

User Name	Password	$	Day Monthly Yearly	Start Date	End Date

Web Site:

User Name	Password	$	Day Monthly Yearly	Start Date	End Date

Web Site:

User Name	Password	$	Day Monthly Yearly	Start Date	End Date

Web Accounts

Web Site:

User Name	Password	$	Day Monthly Yearly	Start Date	End Date

Web Site:

User Name	Password	$	Day Monthly Yearly	Start Date	End Date

Web Site:

User Name	Password	$	Day Monthly Yearly	Start Date	End Date

Web Site:

User Name	Password	$	Day Monthly Yearly	Start Date	End Date

Web Site:

User Name	Password	$	Day Monthly Yearly	Start Date	End Date

Web Site:

User Name	Password	$	Day Monthly Yearly	Start Date	End Date

Web Site:

User Name	Password	$	Day Monthly Yearly	Start Date	End Date

Web Accounts

Web Site:

User Name	Password	$	Day Monthly Yearly	Start Date	End Date

Web Site:

User Name	Password	$	Day Monthly Yearly	Start Date	End Date

Web Site:

User Name	Password	$	Day Monthly Yearly	Start Date	End Date

Web Site:

User Name	Password	$	Day Monthly Yearly	Start Date	End Date

Web Site:

User Name	Password	$	Day Monthly Yearly	Start Date	End Date

Web Site:

User SName	Password	$	Day Monthly Yearly	Start Date	End Date

Web Site:

User Name	Password	$	Day Monthly Yearly	Start Date	End Date